Spiritual
Power Tools
Support for Your Soul

by
Jane E. Hart

Center For Enlightenment
www.cfenlightenment.org

Printed in the United States of America
Library of Congress Control Number: 2004091707
ISBN 0-9753047-0-4

DEDICATION~

THIS BOOK IS DEDICATED
TO ALL SOULS WHO ARE
PASSIONATELY STRIVING
TO LIVE IN THE
BRILLIANT RADIANCE OF
THE TRUE SELF.

CONTENTS

INTRODUCTION

When I consciously set out on my spiritual path over thirty-five years ago, I had no idea of the magnitude of the journey I was undertaking. I could not comprehend the changes that would take place in my consciousness and throughout my entire being. I always wished I had a teacher, guide or helpful book to let me know I was on the right track. I yearned to know that I was not alone in this endeavor to be fused with my Higher Self.

I stumbled and fell many times, but somehow, I found the courage and tenacity to keep going. These "Spiritual Power Tools" were forged from the fire of my passion to be free from my lower self. I designed and created them from my desperation to succeed.

While I was in the midst of the intense

struggle to conquer my limited self, I vowed that if I were victorious, I would do everything I could to help others equally committed to overthrow their lower self and win this revolution in consciousness.

The "Spiritual Power Tools" are designed to enable you to work in the best interest of your soul. They will move you into an entirely new state of awareness. Use these Tools to become fully conscious of your God-Self.

In this book, you will learn exactly what is required to move out of your present state of mind. You will be provided with a step-by-step outline that will lend clarity and simplicity to your spiritual quest. It is up to you, however, to take responsibility for your soul's evolution.

It is my deepest desire and greatest joy to share these Spiritual Power Tools with you. Utilize them to build your new spiritual consciousness and discover yourself as Pure Being.

With loving support,

Jane E. Hart

INTRODUCTION TO SOUL EVOLUTION

Before using your Spiritual Power Tools, it's important to understand how your soul has evolved over many lifetimes. Your soul has been on a challenging pursuit that has brought you to this point in your spiritual growth. The first section of this book is designed to reveal how your soul has been attempting to unfold into full God-Consciousness.

Each chapter will also enable you to comprehend your soul's history and background. You will become familiar with basic principles that will shed light on your next stage of evolution.

Let these ideas be your foundation. Allow them to pave the road for your journey to wholeness. As you use the Spiritual Power Tools in the future, your knowledge of the evolutionary process will give you the courage to use these Tools and to take your steps with confidence.

CHAPTER ONE:

THE SOUL

People use the word "soul" in many different ways. For our purposes, let us define it as follows. The soul is a fragment of God. Through your soul, you are linked with God. In fact, every living thing has a soul, and in that way you are connected with all forms of life. Your soul unites you with God, and with all beings on the planet!

The soul can also be described as an individual portion of the Mind of God. When you develop a line of communication with your soul, your ideas expand and your awareness of all things increases. All solutions to every problem become available to you.

The soul is your True Self. Your true essence is not contained within the physical body, the emotional body or the mind. The soul is the link between God and your physical form.

You probably wonder why your soul exists and exactly what it is doing in the scheme of things. The object of the evolutionary process is to enhance and deepen the soul's awareness. Although the soul is a part of God, it is not yet consciously aware of that amazing fact! It's important to understand how your soul evolved over many eons of time. You may be curious as to how you arrived at your present state of awareness.

The process that propels your soul forward in its evolution is called the Law of Rebirth, or reincarnation. It provides the opportunity for your consciousness to explore and experience the vast arena of life. Through reincarnation, your soul ultimately arrives at the complete and conscious revelation that it is one with God.

Obviously, you need many incarnations and a variety of opportunities to come to the full awareness that you are a God-Being. One lifetime isn't enough to accomplish this goal. As your spiritual consciousness develops, you become more aware of your soul. Each incarnation increases your ability to know your True Self that exists in God.

Everyone has a soul that is evolving. Some souls are evolving very quickly, and others more slowly, but all souls are moving ahead! Each of us is waking up to the fact that we are part of God, and have always been a part of God.

Every day, seek to merge your consciousness with

the awareness of your soul. Life will start to feel more fulfilling. You will know on a deep level that you are expressing your divine purpose. As you awaken, you will be more eager to develop even greater aspects of yourself. First, however, your limited ego must be subdued in order to unify, blend and align the soul with its unlimited individual God-Self.

CHAPTER 2:

FROM
INTELLECT TO INTUITION

You have spent lifetime after lifetime developing your intellect. You have explored many amazing features of your mind and have learned numerous things about the world. Now you are ready to use your intelligence in a higher way. You have a craving to understand your soul and are beginning to ask questions about its essence.

You have become intelligent enough to know there is more to you than the limitations you are presently experiencing. At this point you must develop an advanced style of thought, which is your intuition. The intuition is actually a higher faculty of the mind, and it will open up an entirely new world of learning.

Once awakened by your yearning, your intuitive mind begins to activate your consciousness. You may become more interested in spiritual pursuits, or wonder about the meaning of life and your place in the Universe.

The main function of the intellectual mind is to reason things out and to analyze your thoughts, circumstances and surroundings. The purpose of the intuitive mind is to expand your consciousness beyond the scope of day-to-day life.

Developing your intuition is the next phase of your soul's evolution. Up until now, your intellect has dominated your conscious mind, and it has served you well. As you take steps to empower your intuition, your intellectual mind will take second place. Your consciousness will expand, and you will gradually transcend the limitations of your intellect and utilize your intuition.

Intellect can only take you a certain distance along the path to enlightenment. The intuition must be strengthened in order to continue the process. In fact, you could say that intellectual ability is the intelligence of the personality, while the intuitive faculty is the intelligence of the soul. The soul's wisdom is the cornerstone of your spiritual evolution.

When your intuitive mind takes charge, it enables you to have a deeper understanding of your life circumstances. It grants you a wider vision than is available through the small peephole of your intellect. As you transition from intellect to intuition, you will shed your personality attachments and have greater identification with your soul. Daily meditation provides the gateway to your intuition.

For additional support, refer to
Spiritual Power Tools:
- # 1: Meditation (p. 39)
- # 2: Journaling (p. 40)
- # 3: The Spiritual Thermometer
  (p. 43)
- # 7: Guidance (p. 66)

CHAPTER 3:

MEDITATION

Meditation is the most important action you can take to change your consciousness. Meditation is the method of stilling your thoughts. During meditation you change the direction of your energy. Instead of stimulating the brain with information from the senses concerning the outside world, meditation quiets the mind in order to make it receptive to the inner world of the soul. Meditation is vital because it is the process that unveils your True Self and connects it with your God Consciousness.

It is helpful to meditate on a daily basis. Creating a special place in your home, with a comfortable chair and peaceful surroundings, will support this process. You are setting up a vibration and an energy that will empower your meditation.

At first begin meditating for five minutes a day. You will realize just how busy your mind is! Listening to a guided meditation may help you focus. You might even imagine your mind as a tape player. When thoughts dance through your head, see yourself shutting off the tape.

Do not get discouraged! This is a difficult task! Other supportive options could be using a mantra, or saying one word every time your mind begins to wander such as, "God" or "Love." Concentrating on your breathing is another useful centering exercise.

There may be times you prefer to take a walk or practice yoga while meditating. Any action in which you become absorbed and forget yourself is valuable as meditation.

It is normal to be distracted by thoughts when you meditate. Even if you spend your entire meditation pulling your mind away from these distractions, you will soon realize that your efforts are enabling you to control your mind and connect with your soul.

You may feel like nothing is happening during your meditation time, but continue your daily discipline. It is also common to experience "dry spells" after a period of very enriching meditations. Don't get frustrated and think that something is wrong. You have made a commitment and God knows the desire of your heart. In spite of appearances, you are making progress and changing your consciousness. Be assured that something is definitely happening!

In fact, scientists have discovered that different patterns of brain waves are produced during meditation. Also, brain scans have revealed that meditation awakens portions of the brain that are normally dormant in the average person. You have probably heard that humans only use a tiny amount of the brain's capacity. Meditation ignites certain neurons and forges new pathways that literally enable you to think differently.

You have always had the ability to turn on these spiritual faculties, but this is the first time in the history of your soul's evolution that you have desired to "flip the switch." God has supplied you with all the equipment you need to accomplish your spiritual goals! You have always been "wired for spirituality," yet now you are taking the meditative actions that will fire up the mystical areas of your brain.

Your mind is very similar to a computer. When you make a commitment to meditate, it is like you are adding a new program onto your "spiritual hard drive." You are able to use your mind in new ways, just like a computer can do exciting tasks after a new program is installed.

Now imagine God as the internet. Through meditation, you have already installed the program that will allow you to connect with the "God internet." Now you can "download" all sorts of data that is valuable to your soul.

Meditation prepares a channel for your brain to

God Computer

GOD
Main Computer

Access to All
Universal Information

**Meditation is the direct line
to the Main Computer.**

YOU
Stand Alone Computer

**Intuition interprets the
information and brings it
into your consciousness.**

receive the knowledge that is stored in the Universal Mind of God! Any piece of information you need is readily accessible from that direct line of communication. Your brain will be infused with creative new ideas. You will have far more options than were previously available to you before you "upgraded your computer."

On the spiritual level, your "upgrade" allows you to move from the limited human world of the third dimension into the soul's unlimited fourth dimensional realm. These dimensions will be further explained in the next chapter.

You can see why meditation is so important. It is the avenue to Universal Wisdom and the power that frees your soul!

SENSATIONS YOU MAY EXPERIENCE DURING OR AFTER MEDITATION

- You may feel a cool sensation on your forehead, as if you had menthol rub between your eyebrows.
- You could experience a slight tension or pressure between your eyes.
- You might feel as if a stream of energy is moving over your forehead.

- The top of your head may heat up.
- The top of your head could feel itchy.
- You may see white or colored lights when your eyes are closed.
- You may feel a bright light in your face, which is brighter than the actual light in the room.
- You might feel as if you are expanded beyond your body, or above your body.
- You may be unable to think in your normal way and your brain may seem blank. Later, you could be aware that information has been "downloaded," and you have instantaneous and complete understanding of the information.

These possible experiences are all signs that your "spiritual wiring" is being "upgraded" and your new brain centers are being activated.

It is useful to know that intuitive energy vibrates at a higher rate than your intellectual mind. When you first contact your intuition, you might feel jittery, anxious or unsettled. This is completely normal. Soon your nervous system will adapt to this increased level of vibration, and you will access intuitive information with serenity and poise.

For additional support, refer to
Spiritual Power Tools:

CHAPTER 4:

MOVING FROM THE THIRD INTO THE FOURTH DIMENSION

Meditation prepares your consciousness to move beyond the third dimension of human comprehension, into the fourth dimension of spiritual knowledge. During your various incarnations, you have explored the third dimension and are quite familiar with it. You have realized you can create a desire, and then work to fulfill it. In this way, you've experimented with many facets of your human identity.

Eventually, you begin to understand that searching for happiness outside yourself brings difficulty. The bad always comes along with the good. You realize that you are limited by pairs of opposites. By their nature, opposites are bound together and can't be separated. You are happy, and then you are sad. You feel safe, then anxious. You experience the glory of being alive, and then are painfully aware that one day your body will die. The opposites and the third dimension are under the Law of Reincarnation and Karma.

By now, you are at the point of soul evolution where you are tired of being batted back and forth by the opposites. In fact, you are losing interest in the third dimension and find it less compelling. You might even be bored and unfulfilled in a subtle, yet powerfully unsettling way. Your mind is wrestling to discover the true purpose of life.

These feelings are signs that you are ready to move ahead in consciousness. This is your soul's way of encouraging you to seek out the uncharted area of the fourth dimension and to live from the higher perspective it provides. Connecting with your soul is the only thing that will satisfy your indefinable yearning and fill the void within you.

Although you have longed for material possessions and yearned for certain types of experiences, your desires have also kept you chained to the third dimension, and to the Law of Reincarnation. The Universe wants to fulfill each of your third dimensional desires, yet this process has kept you going around in circles. Now you are beginning to realize that the energy of desire is very powerful and should be used wisely. If you replace third dimensional desires with the single fourth dimensional passion to know

18

your soul, your one-pointed focus will assure your success. The power of that spiritual desire will rocket you ahead, and ultimately free you from the third dimension and the Law of Karma.

Moving into the fourth dimension is a gradual process that aligns you with your Whole Self. As this shift occurs in your consciousness, you begin to see, hear and experience things differently. You will move out of the third dimension slowly but surely. Over time, you will become fully aware of your God-Self.

In the third dimension, you are karmically bound to the opposites. In the fourth dimension, you transcend the opposites and their limitations.

To help you understand the difference between these two states of consciousness, here is a list of how your life will be improved when you live on the fourth dimension.

Third Dimensional Consciousness	**Fourth Dimensional Consciousness**
You cannot turn off your mind.	You have mastered the art of turning off your mind.
You identify with your limited self.	You identify with your Unlimited Self.

You identify with the intellect.	You identify with your intuition.
You mind is out of control.	You can quiet your mind at will.
You think happiness lies in the outside world.	You understand happiness exists within you.
You live in the opposites.	You live beyond the opposites.
You feel powerless.	You feel empowered.
You are either worried about the past or future.	You are fully present to the moment
You are dominated by your emotions.	You are in control of your emotions.
You live in fear.	You live peacefully.
You hold grudges.	You know how to forgive.

You are afraid to make decisions.	You know when to take action.
You are afraid of change.	You welcome change.
You feel out of harmony with yourself.	You are in harmony with yourself.
You feel separate and alone.	You feel secure and complete.
You are afraid of silence.	You enjoy silence.
You are self-absorbed.	You are unselfish and understand your responsibility to all humanity.

When you compare these two states of consciousness, you see the vast difference between them. As a person in the third dimension, you look at life through a tiny peephole in a fence, and you have a narrow perspective. When you are in the fourth dimension, you are entirely above the fence. You always have an unlimited view in all directions. This higher vision provides knowledge that enables you to participate in the unfolding of your soul's purpose.

For additional support, refer to
Spiritual Power Tool

- # 1: Meditation (p. 39)

CHAPTER 4A

COMMITMENT

The first step on this exciting spiritual adventure is to make a commitment to participate in your soul's evolution. At this point of your growth, you are less interested in the third dimensional world. You are becoming more intrigued with the soul's fourth dimensional realm of intuition and enlightenment.

Your soul has been evolving for eons, yet this is your first opportunity to consciously make the choice to move out of the third dimension into the fourth dimension. Once your consciousness has expanded to include the fourth dimension, you will become totally aware of God existing within you.

The moment you choose to take responsibility for your soul's progress, a new vibration and energy will flow into your life. You are making a profound decision that will reprioritize and restructure everything in your world.

Remember that without a strong commitment, nothing can be accomplished. Your personal determination is the driving force that propels you forward toward your spiritual goal.

By committing to work in the best interest of your soul, you have made a powerful request that will resonate throughout the Universe. You can trust that you will get the support you need for your journey.

If you are prepared to make a commitment to your Higher Self at this time, please sign below.

I am ready to move into fourth dimensional consciousness.

_____

SIGNATURE

CHAPTER 5:

YOU ARE 1/10 CONSCIOUS AND 9/10 SUBCONSCIOUS!

In order to understand the evolutionary history of your soul, you must first recognize that you are 1/10 conscious and 9/10 subconscious. All of your past life memories and experiences, as well as the talents you have developed in previous incarnations, are stored in the subconscious mind.

The part of your mind that is 1/10 conscious makes decisions and draws conclusions based upon limited knowledge. It only has access to a small segment of your inner resources. To realize your wholeness, you must become aware of the information hidden in your subconscious.

These two levels of consciousness are separated by a veil. Subconscious emotional reactions that are rooted in past lives can surface and pass through the veil. They impact your present circumstances by causing you to think and behave in baffling ways.

To help you understand this concept, imagine an iceberg. A small fragment is visible above the water. The vast majority, however, lies underneath the surface, hidden from view. This concealed section is very treacherous. It can sink a ship as solid as the Titanic. Believe it or not, your soul is very similar to an iceberg! You are only consciously aware of a small portion of your entire self. Your thoughts and behaviors are mainly dominated by unseen forces, which are entrenched in your subconscious.

As your intuition develops through daily meditation, you gain the ability to look below the surface of your conscious mind into the depths of your soul's history, which has been unavailable to you until now. This is the first time in the evolution of your soul that you have the opportunity to integrate subconscious material into your conscious awareness.

As you assimilate these subconscious pieces, you become 2/10 conscious and eventually 3/10 conscious. Ultimately, you will become 100 percent conscious of your whole being and will have complete understanding of your soul. This is the process you must undertake to uncover the Real Self.

For additional support, refer to
Spiritual Power Tool
- # 1: Meditation (p. 39)

My consciousness is like the iceberg:

1/10 conscious (visible)

9/10 subconscious (hidden)

Thank You, God,
for aligning my
conscious,
subconscious and
superconscious mind.

© Ralph A. Clevenger/CORBIS

CHAPTER 6:

THE PROCESS FOR CONSCIOUSLY UNVEILING YOUR SOUL

God uses the intuitive equipment you have developed in meditation to reveal the subconscious blocks that keep you from spiritual enlightenment.

As this process begins, you will be guided and directed to those things stored in your subconscious mind that get you stuck in negative patterns.

You have certain soul issues that need to be balanced and healed as you move into the fourth dimension. These problems have troubled you in many past incarnations and have resurfaced lifetime after lifetime.

If you return to the "soul as an iceberg" metaphor, you could imagine your intuition as an ice pick. During meditation, your intuition goes to work chipping away at your subconscious. Chunks of information will float to the surface of your conscious mind. This knowledge gives you a new vantage point. You now have the option to think and behave in different ways. With each awareness comes the responsibility to alter your actions. This is how to work in the best interest of your soul.

Once you have consciously assimilated and dissolved a subconscious "ice chunk," your intuition will work to free another piece of that soul issue. A soul issue is too large to overcome all at once, yet is gradually healed over time by this spiritual procedure.

As you make this transition in consciousness, you are beginning to shed your ego. Your limited personality will have less hold on you. You will observe your life from a new vantage point. You will gain the perspective of your soul and it will be easier to remain emotionally detached from your problems. With less emotional drama, you can make wiser decisions.

Transcending the ego is the next step in your spiritual evolution. Your ego is rooted in the third dimension, which is ruled by emotional drama and life in the opposites. You are basically a powerless puppet to the energies of the third dimension and your subconscious mind. Your ego is only 1/10 conscious, although it believes itself to be all-powerful. The intuition breaks the ego's illusion, revealing just how vulnerable you are to the manipulations of subconscious forces. This is a rude awakening!

Even though you want to be free, your ego is afraid of losing that illusion of control. Your lower self will fight with your soul and resist these changes of consciousness. You may end up feeling pulled in two directions. Your ego wants you to stay the same and remain in the third dimension. It might convince you that moving ahead is frightening, that you're too weak to do it, or that the whole process is a waste of time.

Meanwhile, your soul is magnetizing you toward the fourth dimension. A new type of energy is flowing into you. You might feel nervous, disoriented, uncomfortable or overwhelmed. This is natural as your body and mind become accustomed to this higher rate of vibration. You are learning to coordinate and balance the energy of your soul.

Your old ways of thinking are being dislodged. The new patterns are not yet fully established in your consciousness, however. At this point, you are vacillating between the third and fourth dimensions. Your perseverance and discipline must prevail. You are no longer getting satisfaction from the third dimension, but can't fully function in the fourth. You'll often find yourself getting stuck in old thought patterns and outmoded ways of handling situations. Thankfully, you will quickly catch on to the tricks of your lower self and realign your energy with that of your higher consciousness.

While information is bubbling up from your sub-conscious mind, revelations are streaming down into your conscious mind from the superconscious mind, which is Universal Mind of God. Your superconscious supports the process of healing your subconscious soul issues. You will glimpse the bigger picture of your existence, and the possibilities that will exist when your soul is fully awakened and healed.

You can see that as you advance on your path to higher consciousness, energy flows through two channels. The superconscious shines a spotlight down upon you, while the subconscious sends information up from the depths of your soul. The Light of the superconscious penetrates your mind like a laser beam. This higher vibration inspires and empowers you to work on the subconscious pieces that rise up to your conscious mind. This two-part purification process may excite and stimulate you. It is also normal to feel pressured and stressed as these two powerful vibrations simultaneously combine with your conscious awareness.

Your consciousness is trying to expand as quickly as possible to accommodate all the new energy and infor-mation. It is vital to release your fears and limitations so you can easily grasp the new ideas that are sprouting in your consciousness. As was mentioned before and bears repeating, this spiritual procedure allows you to become 2/10 conscious, then 3/10 conscious, and finally fully conscious of your entire soul!

For additional support, refer to
Spiritual Power Tools:

- # 1: Mediation (p. 39)
- # 2: Journaling (p. 40)
- # 3: Spiritual Thermometer (p. 43)
- # 4: Seven Steps for Successful Life
    Transitions (p. 47)
- # 5: Support After Completing the Seven
    Step Process (p. 59)
- # 6: Dissolving Your Emotional Pain (p. 63)
- # 8: How to Stay on the Transformation
    Track (p. 69)

CHAPTER 7:

Spiritual Detoxification

When you desire to move into the fourth dimension, you are seeking a transformation at the deepest level of your being. You are asking for the healing of your mental, emotional and physical bodies. Once you begin to purify your subconscious mind through meditation, rancid soul memories arise in your consciousness. Old modes of thinking are being dislodged and replaced by new revelations. Yet the leftover fears are unhealthy and must be expelled. As these ancient programs are cleansed out, you are likely to feel uncomfortable as the healing takes place. This is due to the "toxins" that are released during the transformation process.

Anxiety also is created because your mind has been used to a certain rate of vibration. The changes that occur through meditation cause a commotion in your consciousness. Your soul sees this as invigoration, yet your ego perceives it as a dreadful disruption. This type of fear must also be overcome in order to embrace the new energy.

At this time, your continued commitment to meditation is extremely important. All these chaotic emotions are actually helping to move your consciousness. Meditation stirs up issues, but it also brings the knowledge and revelations that heal these issues once and for all.

There are many physical and emotional symptoms you may experience which signal that the spiritual procedure is at work and "toxins" are being released. Here is a list of possibilities that may occur.

Getting a cold or sore throat
Having diarrhea
Breaking out in a rash
Waves of heat or cold throughout the body
Tingling sensations
Involuntary rapid or deep breathing
Weight gain or loss
Change of eating patterns
Physical shaking or rocking
Bursting into tears or laughter for no apparent
       reason
Feeling nervous or panicked
Being confused or disoriented
Sudden energy drain or surge

Shifts in sleep patterns
Strange dreams or nightmares

Even though detoxification isn't fun, it is actually a positive sign. It means you are healing at a rapid rate of speed. Just remember that circumstances may appear to be disorderly as your life is being restructured and realigned. Keep your mind open and accept the timing and wisdom of the Universe.

You will emerge on the other side feeling lighter and happier. You will be invigorated and accomplish tasks with less effort and stress. You will feel more in charge of your life than you ever did before! The negative energy you have just released has bogged you down for years. A positive, uplifting vibration has taken its place.

CHAPTER 7A

SUMMARY OF STEPS YOU MUST TAKE
TO ASCEND INTO THE FOURTH DIMENSION
AND TO WORK IN
THE BEST INTEREST OF YOUR SOUL

SPIRITUAL STEP	RESULTS
1. Commitment to work with your soul	Starts the process of unfolding your soul awareness
2. Meditation	Quiets your mind
3. Observe and manage your emotions	Allows for clear thinking and right action
4. Become less dependent upon the intellect	Develops the intuition
5. Release your desires	Stops future karma
6. Forgiveness	Only way to erase past karma and stop future karma
7. Let go of the ego	Empowers your soul

INTRODUCTION TO SPIRITUAL POWER TOOLS

Now that you are familiar with the idea of soul evolution and how it works, you are ready to learn about the various "Spiritual Power Tools" that will assist you in constructing a soul-infused life.

Study these Tools, and incorporate them into your life. You might resonate more deeply with some Tools, and use them more frequently. On the other hand, certain Power Tools may not spark your interest. It is possible that particular techniques aren't right for you.

If you experience strong resistance to a Power Tool, however, it is important to challenge your feelings. After exploring your initial reactions, you will likely discover that the troublesome Tool offers surprising spiritual assistance and becomes your most valued resource.

SPIRITUAL POWER TOOL #1:

MEDITATION

Meditation is the most important Power Tool that you can use on your spiritual journey. The details of meditation are thoroughly explained in Chapter 3. Keep this Spiritual Power Tool handy and use it often! Meditation is the devise that connects you to your soul, and supplies the spiritual electricity that energizes all the other Power Tools.

SPIRITUAL POWER TOOL #2:

JOURNALING

As you meditate and begin to work with your soul to unravel the mysteries of your subconscious mind, writing about your spiritual process will help you immensely. Journaling assists you in focusing your thoughts and allowing intuitive information to arise in your consciousness. Journaling can provide you with revelations and new pieces of understanding that would not come in other ways.

Write down thoughts, images or feelings you experience in meditation. Going back later and reading what you have written can spark surprising insights. Your journal will become an important resource. It will help you remember how your Higher Self answered questions and guided you to right actions. This will help you build confidence in your intuitive abilities.

Journaling can get you to the root of a problem quicker than talking about it, or trying to figure it out in your head. It facilitates a flow of consciousness that opens up channels that disclose hidden information. Write whatever comes to mind. Sometimes you will automatically write your own answers. If you write ideas that seem to be strange or unrelated to your issue, don't censor yourself. This is a process of self-discovery. Soon you will see certain patterns or themes that lead you to clear understanding of deep-seated issues.

You will utilize the Power Tool of Journaling during meditation and the Seven Steps to Successful Life Transitions. You might also use Journaling while working with other Power Tools, such as the Spiritual Thermometer, How to Stay on the Transformation Track, and even during Spiritual Detoxification.

Here are some Journaling questions that will spark solutions when you are caught in the drama of a life situation.

1) What emotions are you feeling?

2) Who or what pushed your buttons?

3) Does this always happen to you? Is this a pattern in your life?

4) What is your soul trying to tell you?

5) If you were guided by your soul, rather than being run by your ego, how would you

handle things differently?

Every problem in life is here to support your soul's evolution. Journaling will reveal the wisdom behind your muddled motives and chaotic circumstances. As you learn about your subconscious secrets, you will make better choices and further your spiritual growth.

SPIRITUAL POWER TOOL #3:

THE SPIRITUAL THERMOMETER

The Spiritual Thermometer is the Power Tool that will help you control your thoughts and manage your emotions. You can only contact your intuition and your Higher Self when you are in a state of "Clear Thinking." It is important to measure the quality of your thoughts before you make any life decisions.

You cannot think clearly when you are drowning in emotional drama. You also don't want to pollute new opportunities with old issues. The Spiritual Thermometer will help diffuse subconscious energy so it won't explode later and cause you future problems.

Your fears, doubts and anger arise for the purpose of being released from your consciousness. You must resolve your negativity so it does not interfere with your decision-making skills. Your "Clear Thinking" will give you the confidence to discern the best options.

On the Spiritual Thermometer "5" is the middle of the scale. It represents an average state of mind. When you sink "below the 5," you get into your limited self. You are

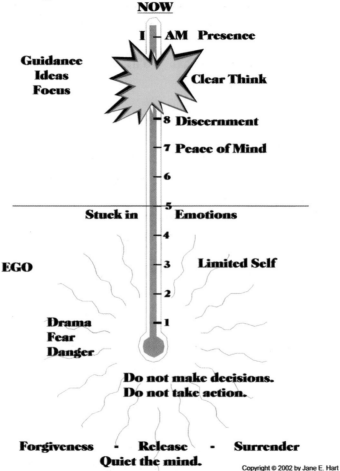

Spiritual Thermometer

NOW

I — AM Presence

Guidance
Ideas
Focus

Clear Think

— 8 Discernment

— 7 Peace of Mind

— 6

— 5

Stuck in Emotions

— 4

EGO

— 3 Limited Self

— 2

Drama
Fear
Danger

— 1

Do not make decisions.
Do not take action.

Forgiveness - Release - Surrender
Quiet the mind.

Copyright © 2002 by Jane E. Hart

44

ensnared in negativity, emotional drama and chaotic thoughts. Do not take action when you are "below the 5!" No problems will be solved from that state of consciousness.

When you are in the midst of an issue, consider how you register on the Spiritual Thermometer. For instance, feeling slightly frazzled would be a "4," but thinking your life is a living hell with no hope of change would definitely be a "1!" This recognition is a valuable step. Evaluate where you are at, and honor that level of emotion. By allowing your present emotional state to be OK, no matter how ravaged you feel, you are on your way to healing. In this way, the Spiritual Thermometer engages your mind just enough to take a step back and look at the situation with some degree of objectivity.

Every problem in life is here to support your soul's evolution. Unless you have a challenge, you will never know your capabilities. Your problems are not awful. They are the most wonderful tools designed to push you forward! Make up your mind as to how long you will be negative about a situation. If you choose an hour, worry all you want for that 60 minutes, then let it go and be open for the solution and the spiritual lesson behind the difficulty. This is how you can work in the best interest of your soul.

It is critical to have an arsenal of positive thoughts so you are prepared for these challenging circumstances.

Examples of affirmations could be, "I have the strength to overcome all obstacles," or "My soul gives me the courage to resolve this problem." It is also helpful to cultivate spiritually supportive friendships with those who will encourage you to lift your thinking "above the 5."

Daily meditation is necessary in order to tap into those higher states of consciousness at levels 6, 7, 8, 9 and 10. You will gradually find yourself calmer in the face of difficulties, and more capable of discerning the actions that support your soul's evolution.

If you remain stuck in an emotional quagmire and cannot get "above the 5," it is time to use your next Power Tool – the Seven Steps for Successful Life Transitions.

SPIRITUAL POWER TOOL # 4:

SEVEN STEPS FOR SUCCESSFUL LIFE TRANSITIONS

This Spiritual Power Tool is designed to help you through the process of changing your consciousness as portions of your subconscious are revealed to you. Any person, place, emotion or idea that limits you must be released so that you

7. Completion

6. Review and Release

5. Forgiveness

4. Disappointments and Difficulties

3. Unfulfilled Hopes and Missed Opportunities

2. Good Times

1. Thank You, God

may remain open to new energy. This simple, yet profound, system will also help you through any type of change that may occur in your life, including divorce, deaths, moving or career changes.

You can use the Seven Steps to release anger you are holding about a person. You can also forgive yourself

the person or circumstance, and how this experience has been important to you. Write your ideas as you think of them.

Journaling Ideas for Step 1

1) **What are you thankful for regarding this relationship or situation?**

2) **What have you gained from the relationship or situation?**

3) **How has this person or circumstance been important in your life?**

Step 2: Good Times

On this step, reflect on the positive side of your experience. Recall the help and support you and the person gave each other. Remember the fun you had and the joy you shared. Fondly reminisce about parties, happy events, vacations and unique occasions. Stimulate your memory by looking at photographs or listening to special songs.

By processing and releasing the good times, you

will be open to even greater good in the future. If you honestly can't think of anything pleasant or redeeming, give yourself permission to move forward to the next step.

Journaling Ideas for Step 2

1) How did this person or situation bring joy to your life?

2) List the happy times you remember.

Step 3: Unfulfilled Hopes and Missed Opportunities

Now is your chance to ponder the could-have-beens, the would-have-beens and the should-have-beens. Think about what you wished you had said or done, and what you hoped the other person had said or done. Acknowledge your feelings of loss regarding your lack of fulfillment. This step is likely to bring up powerful emotions of sadness, anger or guilt. Don't be afraid to experience and journal the intensity of your feelings, since this is precisely your road to healing.

Unfulfilled desires keep you in a vicious cycle of obsessive thought. By recognizing and releasing your hopes and dreams, you diffuse the emotional energy attached to them. Whether you realize it or not, your future is created by your past and present desires.

Journaling Ideas for Step 3

1) How did you expect the other person to behave, or what outcome did you expect from the situation?

2) How do you wish you had behaved?

3) What did you most want from the other person or situation?

4) What remains unfulfilled regarding this person or situation?

Step 4: Disappointments and Difficulties

Your work on the Third Step of Unfulfilled Hopes

will naturally lead to a greater exploration of your negative feelings. Continue to remember the difficulties you faced. Journal as you think about what happened and how these events changed the way you feel about yourself and the other people involved. Consider how your expectations of the person or situation failed you.

Don't judge your emotions if they don't seem to make sense. For instance, you might feel angry with someone who died, even though you had a positive relationship, or you feel ashamed at the depth of your grief over a small situation. It is important to let everything come to the surface in order to cleanse it out of your consciousness.

At times it could feel that you are drowning in emotions that are confusing and overwhelming. You might feel you will never get through to the other side. It is essential to know that you are in the midst of a process that has a beginning, middle and an end. Even though it is challenging, confronting your intense emotions will heal you. The Universe can transform that negative energy into powerful fuel for your future happiness.

Journaling Ideas for Step 4

1) Why are you angry, sad or resentful with this person or situation?

2) **List specific incidents that caused you disappointment.**

3) **What was the greatest challenge your encountered?**

4) **What decisions, attitudes or beliefs do you now have because of these disappointments? How do they affect your life?**

Step 5: Forgiveness

On this step, actively choose to move beyond the pain. Make the decision to accept that the experience happened. You can, however, release your concepts as to why it happened and how it might affect your life in the future. Forgiveness takes time because you are working through all the emotions from the four previous steps.

As you attempt to forgive, you may realize your ego is hanging onto bitterness. Remember that righteous anger drains your energy so you have no fuel to ignite new life possibilities. Relinquish your feelings of resentment, resistance and revenge! Forgiveness transforms negativity and bridges the distance between yourself and others. Most importantly, forgiveness is the only way to erase past karma and to stop future karma from occurring.

In addition to forgiving the person in meditation, you might ask for the person's forgiveness as well. It could be necessary to forgive yourself for your part in creating the circumstances.

An example of a forgiveness meditation could be visualizing light filling your heart. See yourself standing by the fire of love with the person you are forgiving, as you watch your pain and anger burn in the flames. Feel joyous, knowing you are both free from the destructive energy that was between you.

You may even like to create a personal ritual that symbolizes your willingness to forgive. Maybe you could burn the pages of your journal. You could toss stones into a river, lake or ocean. Each stone could represent a good time, unfulfilled hope or challenging experience.

Whether you process your Forgiveness Step by means of meditation, journaling, ritual or a combination of these techniques, you will know you have completed this step when your mind feels at peace.

Journaling Ideas for Step 5

1) **What is the hardest thing to forgive regarding this person or situation? Why?**

2) **How will your lack of forgiveness affect your life in the future?**

3) **What is causing you not to forgive?**

4) **How will your life improve if you do forgive?**

Step 6: Reviewing and Releasing

The Sixth Step gives you time to review your progress. You are preparing to fully release your memories, both positive and negative, as well as your dashed hopes, broken expectations and disappointments. If you feel resistance, go back and revisit some of the earlier steps. When you are ready, visualize the person having experiences that are meaningful and fulfilling. If you are releasing a challenging situation, imagine events coming into alignment that allow for a smooth transition. See yourself happy and at peace in your new circumstances.

The Step of Release gives you the freedom to look at your life differently and make new choices.

Journaling Ideas for Step 6

1) List the positive events you can imagine happening for the other person.

2) Write how this difficult situation could be harmoniously resolved.

3) How will letting go change your life for the better? Outline positive changes you can anticipate.

4) Is there anything you are holding inside that you are afraid to address? If so, what is it?

Step 7: Completion

Completion is the final step of this process. Create closure in a way that is significant for you. Perhaps you can say a powerful prayer such as, "I am grateful for all the lessons and growth that have come through this experience. I am now ready to open myself to new horizons that offer many exciting alternatives!"

This is an important occasion. Celebrate and acknowledge the spiritual work you have accomplished. Now you can eagerly await your new opportunities.

Journaling Ideas for Step 7

1) **How do you see your circum- stances differently now that you have uncovered information by means of this Seven Step process?**

2) **Do you feel inwardly resolved and ready to complete this process?**

SPIRITUAL POWER TOOL #5:

GUIDANCE AFTER COMPLETING THE SEVEN STEP PROCESS

Completing the Seven Steps releases old emotional patterns and creates a reservoir for new energy to flow into your life. You will be presented with a vast array of options. Here are some changes you may experience:

1) Relationships with spouse, children, parents or friends could shift
2) Change in job or career
3) Moving to a new home or city
4) Lifestyle modifications in terms of new interests, hobbies, or social activities
5) A combination of all of the above

When this new energy enters your consciousness, circumstances may feel out of control. Things that worked for you in the past are not working any longer. You may experience a loss of focus or an inability to concentrate.

Sometimes your enthusiasm for life may disappear. Although it feels like your foundation is cracking, these are actually positive developments. You are being prepared to fully embrace your future possibilities. Your consciousness is being upgraded to allow for the incoming higher vibration.

Here are some ideas that will enable you to move through the challenging parts of the integration process.

1) If life circumstances seem out of control: Take charge of your mind by not allowing it to race in all directions. Remedy this anxiety by meditating and perhaps playing soothing music. Once your mind is calm, ask for guidance. Listen for answers and watch for signals in your daily life that reveal solutions.

2) If you are confused and frustrated: Remind yourself that this is a temporary state of emotional "reconstruction." Your Higher Self is working on your behalf. Breathe deeply; center your mind and say, "Thank You, God! I know and trust that You are helping me, even though I don't know what is going on."

3) If you feel depressed or apathetic: Remind yourself that you are experiencing

divine discontent. Change your perspective by imagining your electrical system has been temporarily shut down so that the Universe can "re-wire" your consciousness. Allow yourself extra rest and naps. Don't push yourself to do as many social activities. Be with people with whom you can "be real" and don't have to put on a façade.

4) If you get into escapist or avoidance behaviors: You might feel like running from your feelings of discomfort by eating too much, overspending, watching lots of television, filling your day with too much activity, and so forth. Sometimes the Seven Step process creates a vacuum. It is important not to fill that void, no matter how bleak or empty you feel. Stick with your daily meditation. Make a list of nurturing activities, such as taking a bath, going for a walk or gardening. In this way you will have alternatives that gently soothe you, yet won't disrupt your "rewiring process." Keep a directory of spiritually supportive friends who will remind you of the amazing soul activation that is occurring within your consciousness.

Regardless of the symptoms you are experiencing during this "in between" time, your feelings are temporary and will eventually be replaced with a new sense of vitality and direction.

SPIRITUAL POWER TOOL #6:

DISSOLVING YOUR EMOTIONAL PAIN

You have been building a connection with your soul by meditating, stabilizing your thoughts, and clearing out your subconscious mind. You are taking the responsibility to guard and protect the bridge to your Higher Self. You are more vigilant of your destructive emotions. Some of these powerful feelings may be:

> Resentment
> Anger
> Jealousy
> Self pity
> Depression
> Guilt
> Shame

Although you may feel the pain acutely, you can also remain somewhat detached from the discomfort. You will be able to identify your emotional reactions and realize what is causing you to respond. Once you gain the abil-

ity to observe your emotions in this way, you can utilize the
following process.

1) **IDENTIFY** the emotion and take responsibility for internal reactions and any of your exter-
nal behaviors.

2) **FORGIVE** yourself for this emotional pattern.
Continuing to criticize yourself will inhibit your
healing.

3) **REMIND** yourself that your soul can overcome and resolve any negative pattern.

4) **RELEASE** the emotional energy.

a) Journal your concern and the feelings
associated with it.

b) Use the Seven Step process to prepare
your consciousness to release the negativity.

c) Affirm that you are releasing the problem
and trust that your healing is taking place.

You can't evolve spiritually if you are repressing, avoiding or denying your emotions. Please realize that your soul is sending signals to help you understand yourself at a deeper level. This is the way to consciously participate in dissolving your emotional pain. You are no longer powerless over these old wounds.

SPIRITUAL POWER TOOL #7:

GUIDANCE

The intuitive mind bestows guidance and helps you to take the correct actions for each life situation. It is essential to start trusting your intuitive guidance. The more you trust your intuition, the better it will serve you. Learning to use your new intuitive "equipment" and being able to interpret the information you receive is important. Be gentle with yourself, however, as it requires time and patience to master these skills.

Here are some guidelines to help develop your ability to listen for and receive intuitive guidance.

1) Still your mind. Don't resist your thoughts; just let them pass through your head. In this way, you create a clean slate in your consciousness.

2) Release any preconceived ideas or emotional investment you have. Listening is difficult if you desire a certain response. You can't truly ask if you think you already know

the answer.

3) Guidance may come from surprising sources. A song on the radio, an idea in a book or movie, the casual comment of a friend, or even a billboard on the highway may provide your answer.

4) Be patient and accept the answer you receive. Don't judge or try to analyze it with your logical mind. Show the Universe you accept the solution that was offered by acting upon it.

When you are asking about an emotional situation, it is challenging to discern whether the answer is from your intuitive mind or from your desires or fears. When you receive information, test your guidance by asking yourself these questions:

1) Is it good for all concerned?
2) Is it moral?
3) Is it going to hurt anyone?
4) Does it demonstrate unconditional love?

Once you take action, release your attachment to the outcome.

Exercise your intuition by starting with relatively unimportant questions:

1. At which restaurant should I eat?
2. At which store is the perfect outfit?
3. Which movie should I see tonight?

If in doubt, keep listening. A sure sign that you are following your intuition is a shift of energy. You will feel empowered and more alive. Your intuition has a unique feeling. Consistent meditation will help you become familiar with this new vibration.

Intuition is an abstract experience, and is quite different from your intellectual decisions. Intuitive awareness is not derived from common sense, value judgment or complex rationalization. When you have an intuitive flash, it will be a sudden insight that will instantly bring complete knowledge and total understanding of the situation at hand.

SPIRITUAL POWER TOOL #8:

HOW TO STAY ON THE TRANSFORMATION TRACK

1. Reaffirm your commitment to your spiritual journey.

2. Meditate at the same time every day.

3. Observe your thinking and vigilantly protect the bridge to your Higher Consciousness.

4. Confront your emotional patterns through journaling.

5. When in doubt, forgive!

6. Ask for guidance and listen for answers.

7. Don't dwell on the past or fret about the future. Remain powerfully present in the moment.

8. Recite the "Prescription For Spiritual Alignment" three times a day.

Prescription For Spiritual Alignment

"I am aligned with the Presence of God within.

I am protected by God's Love, Wisdom, Knowledge and Grace.

The God Consciousness within helps me discover more about who I am.

Thank You, God, for the gift of Spiritual Intuition.

Thank You, God, for aligning my conscious, subconscious and superconscious minds."

About the Author

Jane E. Hart is the founder and spiritual leader for the Center for Enlightenment. The Center began in response to the increased public desire to learn more about karma, reincarnation and soul evolution. Jane believes all souls have within themselves a central point that leads to spiritual mastery. Her purpose is to help all seekers connect with that inner light, which enables them to express their full God potential. Jane's own spiritual search began over thirty-five years ago. Over that time, she has guided hundreds of students to work in the best interest of their souls.

For more information on Jane E. Hart and the Center for Enlightenment, including lectures, classes and tapes, visit www.cfenlightenment.org.